Brother Lawrence's simple but profound messages are vital ones for modern-day America. This book will pierce the superficiality of twenty-first-century Christianity.

—GEORGE GALLUP JR., The George H. Gallup International Institute

This spiritual classic, in modern rendering, will continue to open our eyes wide to the overwhelming and benevolent presence of God.

—MEL LAWRENZ, PH.D., senior pastor, Elmbrook Church;
author of *Putting the Pieces Back Together*

Robert Elmer has crafted a wonderful gift by offering a new, refreshing look at *The Practice of the Presence of God*. May new people be surprised and blessed by this new work of an old friend.

—CHARLES MORRIS, president and speaker,
Haven Ministries

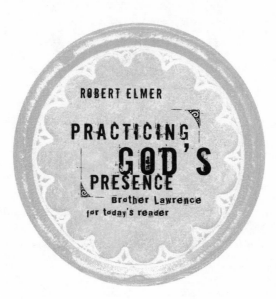

ROBERT ELMER

PRACTICING
GOD'S
PRESENCE

Brother Lawrence
for today's reader

NAVPRESS®

BRINGING TRUTH TO LIFE

OUR GUARANTEE TO YOU

We believe so strongly in the message of our books that we are making this quality guarantee to you. If for any reason you are disappointed with the content of this book, return the title page to us with your name and address and we will refund to you the list price of the book. To help us serve you better, please briefly describe why you were disappointed. Mail your refund request to: NavPress, P.O. Box 35002, Colorado Springs, CO 80935.

The Navigators is an international Christian organization. Our mission is to reach, disciple, and equip people to know Christ and to make Him known through successive generations. We envision multitudes of diverse people in the United States and every other nation who have a passionate love for Christ, live a lifestyle of sharing Christ's love, and multiply spiritual laborers among those without Christ.

NavPress is the publishing ministry of The Navigators. NavPress publications help believers learn biblical truth and apply what they learn to their lives and ministries. Our mission is to stimulate spiritual formation among our readers.

ISBN 1-57683-655-X

Cover design by studiogearbox.com
Cover image by Steve Gardner/Pixelworks
Creative Team: Terry Behimer, Liz Heaney, Arvid Wallen, Kathy Mosier, Pat Miller

Some of the anecdotal illustrations in this book are true to life and are included with the permission of the persons involved. All other illustrations are composites of real situations, and any resemblance to people living or dead is coincidental.

Unless otherwise identified, all Scripture quotations in this publication are taken from *THE MESSAGE* (MSG). Copyright © 1993, 1994, 1995, 1996, 2000, 2001, 2002. Used by permission of NavPress Publishing Group. Other versions used include the HOLY BIBLE: NEW INTERNATIONAL VERSION® (NIV®). Copyright © 1973, 1978, 1984 by International Bible Society. Used by permission of Zondervan Publishing House. All rights reserved.

Lawrence, of the Resurrection, Brother, 1611-1691.
  [Pratique de la présence de Dieu. English. Selections.]
  Practicing God's presence : Brother Lawrence for today's reader / updated and revised by Robert Elmer.
    p. cm.
  Includes bibliographical references.
  ISBN 1-57683-655-X
  1. Christian life--Catholic authors. I. Elmer, Robert. II. Title.
  BX2350.3.L3813 2005
  248.4'82--dc22
                                     2004019468

Printed in Canada

1 2 3 4 5 6 7 8 9 10 / 09 08 07 06 05

FOR A FREE CATALOG OF NAVPRESS BOOKS & BIBLE STUDIES,
CALL 1-800-366-7788 (USA) OR 1-416-499-4615 (CANADA)

CONTENTS

Part 3: SPIRITUAL SAYINGS OF Brother Lawrence

Part 4: IDEAS FOR PRACTICING THE PRESENCE

ABOUT THIS
UPDATED VERSION

The Practice of the Presence of God has been passed down for well over three hundred years in many editions and languages. A favorite of evangelical Protestants as well as Catholics, it has been required reading at many colleges and loved as a personal devotional. As our language changes, we need to reflect once more on what this simple, uneducated monk thought about in the back room of a monastery kitchen or behind a stack of broken sandals. We know from several accounts that although Brother Lawrence had only a grade-school education, he spoke with a genuine common sense that people admired. He was also known for his simple approach to the spiritual life; his honesty, warmth, and humor; and his uncluttered approach to relationships and to faith itself.

But what did he really say, and how did he say it?

In this updated edition I've sought to answer these questions by taking the more dated language of earlier editions and redressing it in the English we speak today, all the while remaining faithful to the original intent. Keep in mind that Brother Lawrence spoke French.

Along the way I've had the privilege of reviewing a

number of different versions, from the 1895 version published by Fleming Revell to several more recent editions from the 1970s, '80s, and '90s. In cases where editors and translators have disagreed over the meaning of obscure wording, I've taken all opinions into account as I searched for the four Cs: clarity, consensus, consistency, and context. Any misinterpretations are mine.

I've also tried to present Brother Lawrence's famous letters in chronological order, though not all scholars agree on the order in which they were written.

This is by no means a word-for-word translation. This is a riskier proposition, a thought-for-thought edition. The risk of such an update is that trying to match fresh metaphors to the author's original intent can sometimes be tricky. On the other hand, the payoff is well worth it when we sidestep obsolete language that once kept us in a fog. The light clicks on! Finally the words make sense. My goal is that this edition will have people saying, "Oh, so *that's* what he meant!" And then, as Hannah Whitall Smith noted in her introduction to the 1895 edition, "What Brother Lawrence did all can do."[1] Can we? The first step is understanding what he really was saying. My prayer is that God will reach a new generation with this message of simple devotion to Jesus Christ— a message clear and uncluttered, like the life of service and love Brother Lawrence modeled.

—*Robert Elmer*

A Short Background

It's interesting how the writings and sayings of an obscure French monk from the 1600s can have such a profound influence on the lives of people today through the pages of a book he never intended to write. Although Brother Lawrence has been called a mystic, an uneducated philosopher, a spiritual innovator, and a saint, he really was none of the above.

He was born Nicholas Herman in 1614 in Hériménal, part of the Lorraine district of France, and we know little of his childhood (not surprising, considering who he was and how long ago he lived). His devout parents could afford to send him to elementary school only, and as a young man he enrolled in the army of Lorraine to fight in the Thirty Years' War.

There's little doubt Nicholas witnessed the worst of war, considering that the Thirty Years' War was a brutal conflict. He was even captured as a spy and nearly executed until he talked his way out of danger and returned to his company. He eventually was sent home after receiving a serious leg injury at the Battle of Rambervillers in 1635. He never fully recovered.

Back home, he served for a short time as a valet to a well-known banker, William de Fieubet, who was treasurer to the French king. The job didn't last long; Nicholas thought himself clumsy and later said he "broke everything."[2] During these years it's likely he sought advice from his uncle, a Carmelite monk, because in 1640, at age twenty-six, Nicholas left home and entered the Carmelite monastery on the Rue Vaugirard in Paris. Without the education (particularly in Latin) to qualify for the higher clerical orders, he entered as a lay brother and was initially assigned to work in the kitchen. He either chose or was given the name Brother Lawrence of the Resurrection.

Brother Lawrence made his formal vows two years later in 1642, yet struggled during his first ten years at the monastery. Though he'd had a spiritual experience and dedicated his life to God at age eighteen, he still wrestled with feelings of unworthiness and didn't particularly enjoy working in the kitchen. Perhaps he still carried a lingering burden of guilt from his days in the war. With time, however, he surrendered himself to God's mercy and came to know the daily closeness of the Lord, what he called the practice of God's presence.

Despite Brother Lawrence's rough exterior and plain-speaking ways, others recognized the profound peace he eventually found in his life. The humble cafeteria worker was sought out for his wisdom and no-frills spirituality by all kinds of people from both inside and outside the monastery, including Father Joseph de Beaufort, vicar general to Cardinal Louis Antoine de Noailles (later archbishop of Paris).

Brother Lawrence's leg injury eventually developed into chronic gout, a painful condition that forced him to limp and ultimately brought about his transfer to the monastery's sandal repair shop where he could sit to work. His illnesses finally caught up with him, and he died in 1691 at the age of seventy-seven.

Soon afterward, Father de Beaufort collected as many letters from Brother Lawrence as he could find. Thirteen were written to a nun, two to a woman outside the monastery, and one to a priest. There might have been many more, but the humble Brother Lawrence had already destroyed most of what he had written, thinking it was of little value.

Father de Beaufort first published his collection in 1692, a year after Brother Lawrence died. It contained the sixteen known letters, a collection of spiritual sayings (called maxims), and a eulogy. Two years later de Beaufort came out with another version containing the notes of four earlier visits with Brother Lawrence. The combined conversations, letters, and maxims became what we know as *La Pratique de la Presence de Dieu*, or *The Practice of the Presence of God*.

Unfortunately, de Beaufort published his little book just as a spiritual whirlwind called Quietism was sweeping Europe. Quietists believed they could achieve perfection through total passivity before God, which involved being absorbed by God and having all effort or desire annihilated. In this divine absorption, they said, sin was impossible because the will was soaked up by God. Among other things, they believed confession and good works were no longer needed.

Church leadership rightfully condemned the doctrine as heresy. However, because Brother Lawrence had also mentioned abandoning the will to God, some people mistakenly linked his ideas to the Quietist movement. In Brother Lawrence's case, however, the resemblance was only superficial because at the core, his teachings directly contradicted those of the heresy. Father de Beaufort even wrote a book in 1697 defending Brother Lawrence's ideas. The result at the time was not entirely positive, though, because publication of a defense implied that the ideas needed defending in the first place.

Although *The Practice of the Presence of God* got off to a slow start in Catholic France, it soon enjoyed a clearly transdenominational appeal. It sold well in England, for example, and John Wesley included it in a special Christian library he put together for new believers. American theologian A. W. Tozer eventually wrote that Brother Lawrence was "well . . . established in the affection of spiritual souls of all denominations and every shade of Christian thought."[3]

More recently, Christian leaders such as pollster George Gallup Jr., pastor and lecturer Ray Ortlund, and Bill Hybels listed *The Practice of the Presence of God* among the most influential books in their spiritual lives.[4] "He wrote very little," said Tozer, "but what he wrote has seemed to several generations of Christians to be so rare and so beautiful as to deserve a place near the top among the world's great books of devotion."[5]

Part 1:

CONVERSATIONS WITH

Brother Lawrence

FATHER DE BEAUFORT met with Brother Lawrence several times while the crippled brother was in his fifties. At that time, Brother Lawrence would have been in charge of maintaining over a hundred pairs of sandals for the other monks at the Carmelite monastery on the Rue Vaugirard in Paris. The meetings with this remarkable man obviously made an impression on the vicar, but he wasn't the only one who was impressed. Another visitor of his remarked that this simple but friendly man was "rough by nature but delicate in grace."[6] Here are Father de Beaufort's recollections.

The First Conversation

August 3, 1666

The first time I met Brother Lawrence was Friday, August 3, 1666. That's when he told me how he had been converted—how God had worked in a great way in his life when he was eighteen years old.

That winter, the sight of a bare tree started him thinking of how it would soon regain its flowers and fruit. That image of the leafless branches never left him—and actually gave him a powerful vision of God's power and providence. In fact, this vision helped derail him from his worldly point of view. It sparked in him a love for the Lord so intense that he could never really tell if it increased in the forty-some years that followed.

Brother Lawrence told me he'd served as a footman to a Mr. Fieubet, a government accountant. He also said that during that time, he was a big, clumsy guy who broke everything. Thinking he could pay for his clumsiness and sins, he decided to enter a monastery, where he would sacrifice the pleasures of his life. But God surprised him by giving him a life of satisfaction instead.

He explained that we should practice God's presence through a continuing conversation with Him, that it would be shameful to trade such a relationship for trivial foolishness, and that we should feed our souls on the highest thoughts of God. We can find deep joy, he said, by simply being with the Lord.

He went on to say that our faith needs revival, and it's too bad we have so little faith. Instead of using it as the guidepost for the way we live our lives, we amuse ourselves with trivial devotions that change every day. Faith, he said, is enough to bring us a complete and mature spiritual walk.

In this walk we ought to give ourselves completely to God, both physically and spiritually, and look for our own satisfaction only in doing His will. Then, whether God leads us into a path of suffering or apparent blessings, it will be the same because we are wholly surrendered to God. We need to hold on to our faith in the spiritual desert when prayer is hard and God refines our love for Him. This is the time for complete surrender to God. A single step of this kind takes us closer to Him.

Brother Lawrence said he wasn't surprised to hear of all the daily sin and misery in the world. Considering what darkness a sinner is capable of, he was actually surprised there wasn't more. He said he prayed for people outside the monastery, but he didn't let it bother him too much because he knew God could set matters straight whenever He liked.

He said that to reach the level of surrender God requires,

we should keep a close watch on the motives and impulses that mingle in both spiritual and physical affairs. God gives seeing eyes to those who truly want to serve and know Him.

Toward the end of our conversation, he told me I was more than welcome to return as often as I pleased—if I really wanted to serve God. If not, then I shouldn't visit again.

THE SECOND CONVERSATION

September 28, 1666

During our second meeting, Brother Lawrence explained how love, rather than selfish goals, had always steered his life. He'd been satisfied with this approach because he'd decided to do everything for the love of God. He was happy even to simply pick up a piece of straw from the ground— for the love of God. All he looked for was God alone— nothing else, not even God's gifts.

So God poured endless grace on Brother Lawrence, the fruit of these gifts being God's affection. But he decided to resist the appeal of these gifts, knowing that the gifts themselves were not God. He knew by faith that God was infinitely greater than the gifts or the feelings he got from receiving them. So a wonderful struggle began: As God gave, Brother Lawrence kept reminding himself how the gift itself was not God. The more God gave, the more Brother Lawrence had reason to focus on the Giver rather than the gift.

Even so, he said it often felt good to play with the gifts instead of looking beyond them to God. Beyond the wonder of it all, it's easy to get carried away. But God is still the Master.

In fact, God repaid everything Brother Lawrence tried to do for Him so quickly and generously that sometimes he just wanted to hide what he did for the Lord. If he never got a reward, he might have enjoyed the pleasure of doing something just for God, not for the reward.

Yet he said he'd been bothered for about four years with fears of being spiritually lost and believed no one would be able to talk him out of those fears. He had finally worked it out in his mind in this way: "I came to the monastery only for the love of God, and I have always tried to work only for Him. Lost or saved, my job will always be to serve God in love. If nothing else, I'll know until the day I die that I gave everything to love Him."

Brother Lawrence realized his troubles came from not applying faith to his walk with God. Once he stopped focusing on himself, he began to find perfect freedom and ongoing joy. He parked his sins in a place between himself and God, while telling the Lord he didn't deserve any favors. Even so, God kept blessing him. Sometimes it was as if God took him by the hand, showing everyone in heaven the undeserving man who had been showered with God's uncounted blessings.

Brother Lawrence said that in order to make talking with God a habit and turn everything we do over to Him, we first have to apply our hearts to Him—and then keep applying them. After a while, it's not hard to get excited about God's love from the inside out.

Brother Lawrence expected pain and suffering after all the pleasant days God had granted him. But he didn't worry about it because he knew in the end he couldn't change anything and God would always give him the strength to handle whatever came.

When he had the opportunity to practice a virtue, he always told God, "Lord, I can't do this unless You enable me." God always supplied more than enough grace.

When he stumbled, though, he simply told God it was his own fault, like this: "Lord, if You left me on my own, I would just keep making the same mistakes, over and over. It's up to You to keep me from falling and to fix what's wrong here." After that he put the pain of his sin out of his mind.

He said that we need to keep it simple between God and us and speak to Him honestly and that if we ask for His help as soon as things come up, God will never fail.

Brother Lawrence then described a recent trip to Burgundy, where he was sent to buy wine for the monastery. This was a challenge for him because of his lame leg and because he had no real head for business. He couldn't even get around on the boat except by dragging himself from cask to cask. He didn't let this or the wine purchase bother him, though. He just told God, "I'm doing Your business." When it was all over, everything turned out fine.

The year before, Brother Lawrence had been sent to Auvergne on the same business. He didn't know how it happened, but somehow everything turned out fine that time too. The same was true of his work in the kitchen, which he strongly disliked. He got used to doing everything there for the love of the Savior, asking for God's grace to do his job well. After a time he became quite skilled in the kitchen, where he worked for fifteen years.

At the time we talked, he was happy working in the shoe repair shop, but he said he was always willing to change, always happy to work at whatever small job was needed, all for the love of God.

Formal prayer times, he said, were really no different than any other times. Of course he went off to pray when the abbot told him to, but he really didn't want or ask for this time because even his most concentrated work didn't distract him from the Lord.

Because he knew he needed to love God in everything, he really didn't need anyone to tell him how to build his life around that truth. He did need someone to hear his confessions, though, and to remind him of his forgiveness before God. Brother Lawrence was always totally aware of his sins, but he didn't let them get him down. He just confessed them to God with no excuses. That done, he returned in peace to his usual practice of love and adoration.

He said he hadn't really described his struggles to anyone. Because he knew by the light of faith that God was with him, he focused all his actions, all his work, on the Lord. Whatever happened, he was willing to lose everything for the love of God. It would be worth it for Him.

Yet troubles always spring from useless thoughts, he said—the kind of thoughts that ruin everything. The trick is to banish them from our thinking as soon as we realize we don't need them for what we're doing at the time or for our Christian walk. Then we can return right back to our conversation with God.

During his first years at the monastery, Brother Lawrence spent his entire prayer time resisting those wandering thoughts and then drifting right back into them. He never had much success praying "by the book" as others did. At first he prayed aloud the way he heard others doing, but eventually he quit that.

Brother Lawrence had asked that he be able to stay a novice monk because his two years as a novice had passed so quickly and he could hardly believe anyone would want to receive him into the order.

He also said he was afraid to ask God for physical discipline. He didn't especially want it, though he knew he deserved it. He also knew that when it finally came, God would also include the grace to get through any physical challenge.

He firmly believed that exercises in self-denial are helpful only if they draw us to know God better in love. After thinking about it for some time, he decided the shortest path to God called for a constant exercise of love—doing everything for God's love.

He also believed there is a big difference between just

doing something as a mind exercise (which doesn't amount to much) and acting straight from the will (which is all-important). In the end, our only business is to love God and delight ourselves in Him. Even the most extreme kinds of physical self-denial—the kinds monks sometimes practiced—couldn't erase a single sin, not one. Instead, we should stop worrying and look for our forgiveness in the blood of Jesus, even as we love Him with all our hearts. As that happens, God showers the most grace on the biggest sinners to prove His indescribable goodness—as well as to build our lives into mercy monuments. Brother Lawrence never really spent much time worrying about dying, or his sins, or heaven or hell. He thought only about doing small things for the love of God, because the high-profile actions were beyond his reach. Then whatever happened to him was okay because it was up to God in the end.

Yet even the greatest pains and joys the world had to offer couldn't compare to what Brother Lawrence experienced in his walk with God. He worried about nothing, feared nothing, and asked God only one favor: "Please don't let me offend You."

His conscience never bothered him, because when he failed, he would go straight to the Lord, saying, "This is what I'll always naturally do if I'm left on my own, Lord." If he didn't stumble, though, he would always give God the credit.

THE THIRD CONVERSATION

November 22, 1666

Brother Lawrence described for me the foundation of his faith: a lofty view of God and a lofty love of God. Once he recognized this, he rejected everything else on the spot so he could live, work, and breathe for the love of God.

But he didn't beat himself up if he somehow got distracted and forgot to focus on God. Instead, he would just confess his miserable sin before the Lord and turn back to Him with more confidence than ever.

In fact, he said, the confidence we have in God pleases Him greatly and brings even more grace. God will never, ever deceive us, and He'll never let someone who is totally dedicated to Him—ready to go through anything—suffer too long.

Because Brother Lawrence had grown in his relationship with God and knew from experience how quickly God would help him, he didn't panic when he ran into temptations. Instead, he would call on God at just the right time, and the temptation would disappear.

Knowing this, when he had a job to do, he didn't worry

about it ahead of time. He knew that when he had to move forward, God would show him clearly what to do, just as clearly as if he were seeing his own face in a mirror. At this point, he'd been following this course for some time, never expecting any trouble or roadblocks. Earlier, though, he'd always worried about the future.

What's more, Brother Lawrence never second-guessed what he had already done and almost never the things he was doing. Even after dinner he could hardly tell you what he'd eaten! In his own simple way he just kept doing all for the love of God, always keeping himself in God's loving presence and thanking Him along the way for guidance.

When anything distracted him from keeping his thoughts on God, the Lord would send a fresh reminder, enough to fill his soul with an overwhelming sense that He Himself was right there. This presence was so strong that Brother Lawrence couldn't keep it to himself—he would have to cry out, sing, and dance.

He said he felt closer to God during the everyday stuff of life than when he hunkered down in formal prayer times that often left him spiritually dry. But, he added, he wouldn't be surprised if he were hit by trials, maybe even serious enough to derail the sense of God's presence he had enjoyed for so long. Even if that happened, though, God's goodness assured him that the Lord would never abandon him. He knew God would always give him the strength to stand against any evil.

So he knew he didn't have to be afraid or worry anyone else about it. (Those times when he had confided in someone, he'd come away feeling worse than ever.) No, Brother Lawrence wasn't afraid because he had already decided he was willing to give up his life for the love of God. That kind of complete surrender was the sure path that God always kept lit.

Living by faith and giving up one's own will are the first steps of that path. Joy follows—a joy that can't even be described. And when the road gets rough, we turn to Jesus, asking for the grace that makes the way straight once more.

Brother Lawrence said many people lose their way by doing penance, trying to work off their sins. The obvious result: They forget about love, the real goal. That's why we don't see much true moral excellence shining through from inside them.

In the end, said Brother Lawrence, it doesn't take skill or a high IQ to come to God—just a heart totally sold out to the Lord, devoted to Him alone.

The Fourth Conversation

November 25, 1667

I've already described some of what Brother Lawrence told me about his walk with God. He spoke about it openly and passionately. This walk, he said, is all about leaving behind forever everything that doesn't lead to God. Doing this helps us get used to a never-ending conversation with Him. It's simple and free.

Brother Lawrence believed all we need is to recognize how God is present in our lives here and now, to focus on Him at all times, to ask for His help when we need it, to search out His will when we're not sure what to do, and to do those things well that He's clearly given us. We can dedicate that kind of work to God before we do it and thank Him when it's done.

Conversation with God also leads us to praise, adore, and love Him nonstop for being so good and so perfect. We should never let our sins discourage us or shut us off. Instead, we should pray for God's favor and be confident that His grace is ours because we rest on the merit of Jesus Christ. It's all about Him, not us.

Brother Lawrence always found God's grace this way, except when his thoughts wandered from practicing God's presence or he simply forgot to ask the Lord for help.

He said God always brings light to our doubts when our only goal is to please Him. If we do grow to become more like Jesus, though, it won't necessarily come from doing something differently on the outside. The change will come when we do things for God's sake instead of our own. Brother Lawrence said it's a shame to see how many people confuse the means with the end, the tool with the goal. He was sad to see how many people were stuck on doing good deeds, which they didn't even do very well because they ended up doing them for all the wrong (selfish) reasons. The best way Brother Lawrence ever found to know God better was to keep doing his everyday business—not to please people, but simply for the love of God.

He said we're fooling ourselves if we think our prayer time has to be different from any other time. It shouldn't be different because we're called to walk beside God in our work times just as much as we would during our prayer times. During his own prayer time, his soul simply recognized God's presence and love. After his prayer time was over and his work time began, he really couldn't tell any difference because he kept walking with God, giving his all to praise and bless Him.

He spent his days in nonstop joy and at the same time

hoped God would send him a challenge to suffer through once he grew strong enough to endure it.

Once and for all, said Brother Lawrence, we need to trust God and put our whole selves in His hands. He will never lead us wrong. We shouldn't get tired of doing little things for God, either, because God doesn't care about the size of the task—only the love behind it. We shouldn't be surprised to fall on our faces at first. Eventually we'll be pleased to find the way that produces worry-free results.

Real religion, he said, is made of faith, hope, and love, and practicing these three puts us in God's game plan. All else is secondary, so we should just use it as a way to reach our goal and splash down in an ocean of faith and love.

Everything's possible when we believe, easier when we hope, and easier still when we keep on practicing faith, hope, and love. We should make it our lifetime goal to become the best worshipers of God we can be in this life . . . as good as we hope to be in eternity.

Brother Lawrence said that when we begin our spiritual walks, we should take a magnifying glass to ourselves to see what we're made of. We'll find that we honestly deserve contempt, that we don't even deserve the name *Christian*. So it should be no surprise if we run into all kinds of nasty troubles and accidents—the kinds that can bring us down, affect our health, or sour our outlooks on life. We're the kind of people God needs to humble with trials from the inside and out.

It should also be no surprise when we go through trouble, temptation, opposition, and denials from other people. Though it seems upside down, we should submit to that kind of grief, taking it on for our own good as long as God pleases. The higher and deeper we want to go with the Lord, the more we'll need to depend on His grace.

Beyond the Fourth Conversation

Collected from other accounts; presumed written by Father Joseph de Beaufort

When another Carmelite brother asked how he'd developed such a habit of knowing God, Brother Lawrence knew he needed to explain. He said that ever since he had arrived at the monastery, he had tried to focus all his thoughts and desires on the Lord. God was his target, his terminus.

At first, as a novice monk, he spent his private prayer hours simply fixed on God. His goal: to convince his mind of God's presence and impress it deeply on his heart. His method: dedicating his convictions and feelings to the Lord while following the light of faith rather than heady philosophical arguments or elaborate meditations. This short, sure exercise helped him know and love God better, and in the process, he resolved to do all he could to live in God's presence and, as much as possible, to never forget his Lord.

As soon as he dedicated his mind in prayer to the highest thoughts of his infinite God, he reported to his job assignment in the kitchen (he was the monastery cook). Once he'd figured out all the details of his work, he spent every possible moment of downtime, as well as before and after work, in prayer.

Each time he began his work, he said to God with the trust of a son or daughter: "O my God, I'm obeying now Your command to pay attention to what I'm doing here. Since I know You're with me, I ask You to please grant me grace to stay and continue in Your presence. Please help me. I give You the work of my hands and the fruit of all my affections."

As Brother Lawrence continued his work, he kept up his close and easy conversation with his Maker, asking for grace along the way while making his work an offering. Each day when he finished in the kitchen, he reviewed how he had done his work. If he'd done well, he thanked the Lord. If not, he asked God's pardon and set his mind right without getting too discouraged about it. Then he slipped right back into his exercise of God's presence, as if he'd never missed a beat.

"By getting right back up after I fall," he said, "and by keeping my walk of faith and love fresh and alive, I've gotten to the place where it would be just as hard for me *not* to think of God as it was in the beginning to get used to the idea."

Because Brother Lawrence found walking in God's presence such an adventure, he naturally recommended it to others. Even more striking, though, was his own example—a stronger argument for walking in God's presence than anything he could ever say. Even just the look on his face, his sweet and calm devotion, couldn't help but touch anyone who saw him.

People noticed that even during the busiest hustle and bustle of the kitchen, he still kept his cool and heavenly-mindedness. He never rushed on the one hand or dawdled on the other. He just tackled each chore in turn—steady, even, and tranquil.

"For me," he explained, "work time is no different than prayer time. Even in the noise and clatter of the kitchen, with different people calling for different things all at once, I still know God's presence with just as much real peace as if I were on my knees at communion."

Part 2:

LETTERS FROM

Brother Lawrence

THESE SIXTEEN letters were written to longtime friends during the last years of Brother Lawrence's life. They were saved by Father Joseph de Beaufort and published shortly after Brother Lawrence's death in 1691.

THE FIRST LETTER

START SMALL:
A LITTLE FAITH GOES A LONG WAY

From the Carmelite monastery on the Rue Vaugirard, Paris
June 1, 1682

My Dear Friend,

I'm writing you to explain how one of our friends and coworkers* feels about living in God's presence. I'm talking about a model for living, an ongoing source of help. We too could benefit from doing what he does.

His ongoing focus for the past forty years? Simply to be with God. His main concern? To do nothing, say nothing, or think nothing that would displease our Lord. His only motive? Pure love for God, knowing our Lord deserves infinitely more.

God's presence has become so much a part of this man's life that for him, it's the source of nonstop comfort and peace. In fact, for the past thirty years the joy has been so intense that once in a while he's had to tone it down around people who wouldn't understand.

If sometimes he gets a little distracted and loses sight of

---

* Brother Lawrence modestly describes himself in the third person here.

that presence, God gently stirs his soul and brings things right back on track. This happens most often when he's busy at work. To remedy the problem, he answers the still, small voice of God in a way that matches heaven's intent. He either lifts his heart toward God or meekly but lovingly bows before Him. Or he might respond with the kinds of words love provides: "Here I am, God, devoted to You 100 percent!" Or, "I'm clay, God. Mold me."

In his heart, he knows this God of love is satisfied with just a few sincere words, and he soon feels as if God were relaxing once more in the deep center of his soul. This kind of experience reminds him beyond doubt that God is always on the throne, right there in the innermost part of his soul, no matter what happens in the world outside.

Here's how you can judge the kind of contentment and satisfaction he enjoys: When he realizes God has placed such a great treasure in his heart, he doesn't have to go out looking for it anymore. He doesn't worry about finding it anymore because God's beautiful treasure is all there, right in front of him. Like an unlimited expense account, he has permission to take and use any part of this treasure he wants.

This man often points out how blind we are and says we should pity those who are satisfied with so little. God, he reminds us, has the never-ending treasure. The problem is that we take in so little of it during our routine, two-minute devotions. We're blind to God's purposes because we unplug the wire that feeds the current of His grace into our lives.

On the other hand, when God comes upon a soul marinated with living faith, He pours out His grace and favors by the bucketful. They can then flow through the person's life like a river that has been kept from its normal course but is suddenly let loose by open floodgates to happily soak everything in its path.

We often stop this holy flood because we think we don't want to get wet. Enough of that! Let's take a look inside ourselves and bulldoze the dike that holds back God's flood. Make way for grace! Let's cash in lost time because we may not have much left. Who knows? If death is tailgating us, we need to be ready. We die only once, and life offers no "do-overs."

So I have to say this again: Let's take a close look at our lives! The clock is ticking, and there's no room for dragging our feet. Our souls are literally at stake.

That said, it looks like you've prepared yourself and followed the right steps so you won't be taken by surprise when you die. I'm really glad you've done the one thing that's most important in life: getting right before God. What's more, we need to keep working at it (see Philippians 2:12) because if we're not moving forward in our spiritual lives, we're moving backward. It's sort of like having our spiritual sails raised to the strong wind of the Holy Spirit: We can be safely sailing forward even when we're asleep. Of course, if our soul-ship hits a few choppy waves, we simply have to wake the Lord, who is resting in the back of the boat. Just like that, He'll calm the sea.

I hope you don't mind that I've laid down all these thoughts on paper so you can line up this truth with what you know from your own experience. And I hope this may help to rekindle the flame of truth in you in case that fire ever burns a little low. Let's always remember our first love, the joy that filled us when we first believed. Let's build on the example of this brother. The world obviously doesn't know him from Adam, but God sure does—and loves him greatly.

I'll pray for you. Please pray for me too.

Yours in the Lord Jesus,
Brother Lawrence

WHY WE DO THE THINGS WE DO: DON'T FOLLOW GOD JUST FOR THE BENEFITS!

Before November, 1685

Dear Reverend Mother,

Today I received two books and a letter from Sister M——.
She's preparing to take her vows as a nun, and she tells me
she would really appreciate your prayers—and of course
the prayers of everyone in the abbey too. I know she very
much values your support, so please don't let her down.

In particular, please pray that she'll take her vows with
only God's love in view and that from now on she'll devote
her life to Him with a single mind and purpose.

I'll send along one of the books she gave me about practicing God's presence. That's what it's all about, really—the
Spirit-filled life in a nutshell. It seems to me that putting the
book's advice into practice will take you far on your walk
with God.

I do know that those who want to know God's full presence need to have their hearts emptied of all worldly stuff.
That's because God never shares a heart with anyone or

anything. So there's going to be some housecleaning if He comes to live in a person's life because He doesn't work to the fullest unless that heart has a "vacancy" sign on its door.

I don't know of a better, sweeter life than an unbroken conversation with God, a life of unlimited free minutes with Him. Only those who are living this kind of life know what I mean. But don't do it just because I'm saying it's sweet. Don't look for the pleasure payoff. It's best to pursue this relationship because we love Him and because it's God's will for us.

If I were a preacher, above all else I'd preach the practice of the presence of God. If I were a spiritual leader, I'd tell everyone to do it—especially because it's so needed . . . and simple as well. If we only realized how much we need God's help and how much He wants to bless us, none of us would lose sight of Him, not for a second.

Listen! Make a solid commitment right now to never let God slip from first place in your thoughts. Resolve to spend the rest of your life with Him—even if it means giving up some of what you think are life's fringe benefits. God has even better ideas. So get serious about following Him; if you do, you'll see guaranteed results.

I'll pray for you in this process as best I can. Please let me know if there's anything I can do for you or anyone else in your abbey.

Yours,
Brother Lawrence

YOU CAN KNOW HIM TOO:
THE GOD FOR ORDINARY PEOPLE

Paris
November 3, 1685

Dear Reverend Mother,

I've received the rosaries from our friend that you passed along for me. But I'm wondering why you haven't told me what you think about the little book I sent you. I'm sure you've received it by now—so go ahead and start putting what it says to work in your life! It doesn't matter how old you are. In this case, better late than never.

I have no idea how Christians can live satisfied lives without practicing the presence of God. I rest with Him in the deep center of my soul as much as I can. I'm not afraid of anything when I'm with Him in this way, and I know I'd fall flat on my face if I turned from Him even a fraction of an inch.

Walking with God this way doesn't tire me out physically. It helps to do without some of the little pleasures of life—things that are okay in themselves but tend to distract us from the Lord. Because in the end, God is not going to let someone who's totally sold out to Him really enjoy any of the other stuff, the trinkets of life. When you think about it, that's really the only way that makes sense.

I'm not saying we need to beat ourselves up or be weird about this. Not at all. Our job is to serve God in holy freedom, which means working faithfully and keeping to our job descriptions without whining or complaining. It also means gently steering our thoughts and minds back to the Lord if we ever get off track.

I have to say, though, that we need to invest 100 percent of our trust in God. Nothing less will do. This means we lay aside all our cares and worries. It might also mean we lay aside some devotions if they get to be just a routine— something we do over and over or for the wrong reasons. Obviously the devotions are great in themselves, but they're really only a means to an end. Once we've grown into the habit of practicing the presence of God, we're with Him. Because knowing Him is our goal, He is our end and we don't need to fall back on the means. We can just keep going deeper with Him in our love relationship. We can ride along with Him in all the ways our spirits invent: by doing something that praises Him or something that shows how much we adore Him. Or by surrendering to what we know God would have us do and thanking Him all the way.

Don't give up because it feels odd or doesn't seem to come naturally. It's common at first to think that pursuing this kind of walk with God is a waste of time. But never mind the bumps in the road. It takes self-sacrifice and an all-out, lifelong commitment.

I depend on the prayers of everyone in the abbey, and yours especially.

Yours,
Brother Lawrence

THE FOURTH LETTER

WHAT DOES IT TAKE TO WORSHIP?
JUST ONE LITTLE STEP AT A TIME

My Dear Lady,

I feel bad for you! It would be wonderful if you could just turn over the hassles of your daily business to our mutual friends and spend the rest of your life focused on worshiping God. After all, God doesn't ask much, just that we:

- Remember Him once in a while.
- Adore Him a little bit.
- Pray for His mercy and compassion.
- Volunteer for tough duty.

And sometimes He wants us to thank Him for all the ways He helps us (and keeps helping us), even when we don't deserve it and even in the middle of our darkest days.

Wrap yourself in His favor as much as you can, like a warm blanket. Lift up your heart to Him when you're eating or when you're in a group of friends. He loves to hear from you, even if it's just a quick "Hello, God—I love You!" or "Wow, Lord. Thanks!"

We don't have to make a lot of noise because He's closer than we know. We don't always have to be in church to be with

God, either. We can remodel our hearts into chapels—the perfect place for a prayer retreat, where we can humbly and peacefully come to the Lord in love without a lot of show. Everyone can do it—some more, some less, of course. God knows.

So let's not waste any time. Maybe He's expecting only a single step from you. Whatever the case, don't back down because life is short. You're almost sixty-five, for example, while I'm pushing eighty. Let's live—and die—with our Lord. Look at it this way: With Him, even the worst day can taste sweet. Without Him, even something like winning the lottery would feel like the worst prison sentence. That's why every mouth needs to praise Him!

Get used to blessing God like this—step-by-step. Get used to falling at His feet, begging for the kind of favor He wants to pour out on us (but that we've done nothing to deserve). Make it a habit to give Him your whole heart and life, not just once but daily. Even if you're on a busy schedule. Every minute of every day, if you can. Don't just go through the motions of worship strictly by the book, locked into the same devotional script all the time. No, try this: Worship God in faith by believing that He honestly wants to know you better. Do what you do out of love. Always remember who you are compared to how great God is.

Don't forget to tell our friends that I'm praying for them as best I can—also that I'd do anything for them and for you.

> *Yours,*
> *Brother Lawrence*

THE FIFTH LETTER

ARE WE CRAZY?
FOLLOWING GOD MAY LOOK WEIRD,
BUT . . .

My Dear Friend,

Though you won't find my lifestyle in a how-to book, I'd still like to know what you think about the way I live. It would encourage me to know your opinion.

A few days ago a well-grounded Christian explained to me what she believed were three stages to a genuine spiritual life. First, it starts out of a servantlike fear of God. Second, it grows in the hope of eternal life. Third, it all comes together in pure love. On top of that, each stage has its own steps.

I haven't followed these three stages at all. My gut feeling was that following them like some kind of road map would only discourage me. So instead, when I became a monk, I figured my only option as a sinner was to give myself totally to God. How's that for simple? And because I loved Him, I gave up everything I owned besides.

When I prayed during my first years as a monk, I thought mostly about death, judgment, hell, heaven, and my sins. The rest of the day I focused on God's presence, even while at work. God was always with me, often as if in my heart. The result: My view of God grew so far beyond what I could imagine to the point where only faith could begin to explain.

Little by little I devoted myself to knowing His closeness—His presence—even during formal prayer times. That delighted me, made me feel as if I were on the right path.

But I have to tell you that my first ten years were rough. I worried about my relationship with the Lord, that it wasn't everything it ought to be. I worried about my past sins. I even worried about the favor God showed me. So I had plenty of ups and downs. And here's the hard part: It seemed as if everything and everybody were against me, sometimes even God Himself! Only my faith kept me going.

I doubted. Who was I to think that God had really blessed me so soon and so much when others struggled a long time with their own spiritual walk? Was I shooting myself in the foot? Was I hopeless?

This tough time didn't drag down my trust in God, but rather it helped me to learn to trust and depend on Him even more. Because just when I thought I was going to have to live the rest of my life feeling constantly down and unworthy, my battered, uptight soul settled down. I changed as my soul discovered real peace from the inside out—a place of rest, a place to belong, an anchor.

Since then I've walked with God simply and in faith. It's

a humble path of love. Day after day I spend my time doing what will please God. When I do this, I hope He'll do what He pleases with me.

I can't really describe how my motives work today, except I want only what God wants. In everything I do, I want His will. It's to the point where I wouldn't take a single step against what He wants. Everything I do is out of pure love for the Lord.

Today I've quit those formal, set prayers, except those that go with being a monk. My priority is to be in God's presence—and stay there. That's where I focus on devotion to Him, a real presence of God. In other words, this devotion is my soul's regular, quiet, private conversation with God. This is where I find joy and how I stay content. Sometimes the joy is so intense that I have to tone it down, and I'm afraid that I might even look silly. Yet I'm 100 percent sure my soul has been with God these past thirty years.

I'm trying not to bore you with too many details, but I should explain how I see myself before my God, my King. I'm a loser—full of faults, flaws, and weaknesses. I've wronged God in so many ways. I've regretted this greatly, confessed it to God, and asked for His forgiveness. What can I do but abandon myself in His hands to do with me what He wants?

But my King is full of mercy and goodness. Instead of making me feel bad, He hugs me with His love and invites me to dinner. He serves me with His own hands and gives me the key to His treasures. He enjoys me and talks to me and treats me like a favorite child. He forgives me and takes away my bad habits without even mentioning them. The weaker I am, the more loved I feel. That's how I feel in His holy presence.

Usually I respond by giving Him my complete attention and affection. I'm often attached to Him more closely than a nursing infant to his mother. To follow that analogy, it's as if I'm at the bosom of God. I can't even describe the sweetness I taste and know with Him. So if I ever have to think about other things (for example, when I'm sick), I'm drawn back by the sweetest emotions. I can't even describe them.

For a contrast, think for a minute on what a great loser I was, rather than on the great favors God did for someone who didn't deserve or appreciate the depth of that mercy. My regular prayer times simply continue the same approach. Sometimes it's as if God is a carver and I'm a stone. I present myself to Him to carve His perfect image in my soul and make me like Him. Other times when I come to Him in prayer, it's as if He lifts up my spirit and I don't even have to try. I'm suspended in and centered on Christ— fixed on Him, my place of rest.

I know that some people think this kind of walk with God is lazy, crazy, or self-loving—something like contemplating one's navel. Call it "holy leisure," maybe. Some people think it might be a happy kind of self-love—except that this close to God, those kinds of faults and old habits (including self-love) have been left far behind. What I used to depend on and live for would drag me down today.

But crazy? Not a chance. Anyone who enjoys God this much wants nothing but Him. Yet if I'm imagining this, it's up to God to fix it. I say let Him do what He wants with me. I want only Him and to be totally His.

So what do you think of all this? Please let me know, as I value your opinion and defer to you as a mature believer.

> *Yours,*
> *Brother Lawrence*

THE SIXTH LETTER

AFRAID?
NOT WHEN WE STAY CLOSE TO THE LORD

Dear Reverend Mother,

Even though my prayers don't amount to much, I promised you I'd pray for you, and I'll keep my word.

Wouldn't it be incredible if we actually found the treasure our gospel talks about? Nothing else would compare—not even come close. Because the treasure is unlimited, the riches only get better the more we focus on the search. So let's not stop searching until we find it.

Finally, Reverend Mother, I don't know what's going to happen with me. It seems as though peace of mind and rest for my soul come to me even when I'm not awake! I would go through suffering for my sins if that's what God required, but all I know is that He's protecting me. In that divine protection, I'm in such a tranquil zone that nothing scares me anymore. What's left to be scared of when I'm with the Lord? I'm hanging on to One who deserves blessings from everyone. Amen!

Yours,
Brother Lawrence

THE SEVENTH LETTER

ON THE MARCH:
HOW SOLDIERS CAN WALK WITH GOD

October 11, 1688

Dear Mrs. N——,

We have an infinitely good God who showers us with an unending supply of grace—the kind of favor we don't deserve. Of course, He knows everything we want or need too.

I have always thought God would allow you to suffer greatly. He tends to show up in His own time when you least expect it. So believe me, you can bank on Him now more than ever. Join me, then, to thank Him for all the favors He grants you—especially for the backbone and the stick-to-itiveness He gives you during your tough times. See? That's a sure sign of the way God is taking care of you. Knowing this, you can lean on Him for comfort as you thank Him for everything.

I also admire the grit and courage of our friend in the army. God's given him a good attitude about a lot of things, even though he's a bit worldly and still has some growing up to do. I'm actually hoping the harsh challenge God laid on him opens the door for some serious soul-searching. In the process, what we think of as bad news may actually help restore him. Here's his chance to totally trust God (who is with him always) and to focus on the Lord when he's in danger.

All he needs to do is lift up his heart a little and remember the Lord. Even if he's marching along in full battle gear, a quick prayer is an act of worship—and God fully accepts that. What's more, prayer doesn't water down a soldier's nerve during the tough times. Just the opposite, prayer builds up his courage.

So he should keep his mind on the Lord as often as he can. If he does, he'll gradually get used to this kind of holy workout, stepping it up in degrees. Think of it as a simple, all-day worship exercise, just between him and God.

Please pass along to him this strategy for focusing on the Lord. It's perfect for a soldier—a must for the kind of guy who is in harm's way every day.

In the meantime, I trust God will give him and his family whatever special help they need.

> *In your service and theirs,*
> *Brother Lawrence*

DISTRACTED DURING PRAYER?
STEPS TO KEEP FROM WANDERING

My Dear Reverend Mother,

What you told me in your last letter doesn't surprise me. You're not the only one who's bothered by a distracted prayer life. In fact, everybody's mind is prone to wander—a lot. But! We're designed so that our wills are in charge. They can pluck those stray thoughts and deliver them up to God.

Yet if we don't start our devotional lives out on the right foot (with control and discipline), we can pick up bad habits. That's when our minds start channel surfing and get distracted with things that don't really matter. Once that happens, it's tough to get back because our minds will drag us through thought-junkyards we never intended to visit.

One way to fix this mess is to come clean before God. Beg Him for mercy and help.

But wait—I'm not saying you should just pile on the words in your prayers, because that can take you right back down a different set of rabbit holes. No, when you bow before God, hold the words back. Imagine you're a crippled beggar in front of a Hollywood mansion and you can't speak.

Make it your business to keep your mind in God's presence. But don't get upset if your mind sometimes wanders and pulls away. Getting upset will only distract you that much more. The job of our wills is to bring us back into a peaceful place. So hang in there; God is full of mercy.

One way to stay collected and regather your mind while you're praying is to keep it on a leash when you're *not* praying. If you develop the habit of staying focused on the presence of God during the day, you'll see it's easier to keep your mind calm during prayer as well. Even if your thoughts do wander a bit, they'll be trained not to wander too far, and it'll be easier to refocus on the Lord.

You know from what I told you before how good it is to practice the presence of God. So let's pray for each other as we dive into Him with everything we have.

Yours,
Brother Lawrence

LOVE FIRST, OR COMMITMENT?
A CHICKEN-AND-EGG STORY

March 28, 1689

Dear Reverend Mother,

Here's my reply to our sister's letter, if you would please deliver it to her. She means well, but she's running out ahead of God's grace, and she needs to know there's no such thing as instant holiness.

Actually, I think you'd be an ideal teacher for her. While we can help each other with our advice, a good example works even better. Every now and then, please let me know how she's doing, whether she's on fire for the Lord, following Him.

We need to keep remembering that pleasing God is our only real job and that everything else is silly and self-centered.

Now, you and I have both lived in monasteries for over forty years. Have we spent that time really loving and serving God? That's what He's called us here to do. Yet sometimes I'm hit with a double-dose of shame and confusion when I think back on everything God has given (and keeps giving) me. I realize how poorly I've used those gifts and the tiny baby steps I've made toward being more like Christ.

But He's patient, and He gives us a bit more time. So let's

get to work. Let's make up for lost time! Let's run right back to God, who's always waiting with open arms and a big hug. Because we love Him, let's turn our backs on everything that's not of Him. It's the least we can do, though He deserves so much more. Let's keep our minds on Him around the clock, trusting Him 100 percent.

There's no doubt in my mind that God is soon going to unload another huge dose of grace on us. It's the kind of grace that gives us the power to serve Him. Without it, we're left with the flat tire of sin. We'll always bottom out on life's potholes without God's real, ongoing help. So let's keep going to Him in prayer.

But here's the rub: How can we pray to Him without actually being with Him? And how else can we be with Him except by thinking about Him a lot? And how can we think about Him a lot unless we've been working on that holy habit?

Maybe you think I'm saying the same thing over and over, and maybe you're right. But this is the best and easiest way I know to get close to God. I don't have any other methods or ideas, but I think the whole world should be doing this.

To love someone, we first have to know that person. To know God, we have to think about Him. Then when we come to really love Him, we'll think of Him a lot . . . and on it goes. Our hearts follow our treasure. Let's keep this truth in mind.

Yours,
Brother Lawrence

WHEN FRIENDS BECOME MORE: KEEPING GOD IN FIRST PLACE

Paris
October 29, 1689

Dear Madame,

I had a really tough time writing this letter to Mr. de N——, and in part I'm doing it now only because you and his wife wanted me to. Could you please address it and send it to him?

It's great to see your faith in God, and my prayer is that He will grow that faith in you more and more. There's no such thing as too much trust in the good and faithful Friend who will never let us down—not here and not in the world to come.

If Mr. de N—— responds to his loss by trusting God, he'll see how the Lord will bring even sweeter friendships into his life. God can deal with our emotions, after all. But it could be that Mr. de N—— was too emotionally attached to the friend he lost. Maybe the friendship became an emotional be-all and end-all. Of course we need to love our friends, but we can't let that affection steal first place in our hearts or replace the love and devotion that belong to God alone.

Don't forget what I told you about always keeping your

mind on God. That means by day and by night, at work or during your off-hours. God is always near you and with you, so don't ignore Him. It would be rude if friends stopped by to visit and you left them alone, wouldn't it? So why do we ignore God? Don't forget Him! Think about Him all the time. Tell Him you love Him. Live and die with Him, because that's our incredible job description as Christians. It's actually our calling, our career—and we need to learn that if we don't know it already.

I'll keep praying for you.

Yours in Christ,
Brother Lawrence

WHERE DOES IT HURT?
GOD WORKS THROUGH PAIN

November 17, 1690

Dear Reverend Mother,

I'm not praying that God will take away your pain. Instead, I'm on my knees asking Him to give you strength and patience to handle it for as long as He decides. Take comfort in the weight of the cross because He will lift your burden when the time is right. There's actually joy in suffering with Him. So get used to it and look to Him for the strength to carry on as long as He feels it's needed.

NonChristians just don't get it. But that's no surprise because they go through hard times as unbelievers, and that's not much to go on. They don't see how God can bring about good through sickness; they just see it as unnatural pain or as grief and angst. But when we believe that God's hand is right there in sickness and we see how He kindly uses it for our salvation, that's when we know we're surrounded by His sweet purpose and His care for us through it all.

I wish you'd understand that God is often closer to us when we're sick than when we're doing fine. In the healing process, don't just trust in your doctors, because God is the ultimate MD. Trust Him totally, and you'll see the difference as you recover.

Sometimes we can actually take longer to recover when we trust in medicine more than the Lord. Don't forget, any treatment will work only as well as God allows. If God sends pain, He's the only one who can cure it. Often He'll go so far as to make us physically sick to cure spiritual diseases. So rest in the arms of the Great Physician of body and soul.

I hear it coming, though: You say, "I'm doing great. I'm close friends with God, spending time with Him all through the day, eating and drinking at His table. What do I know about the misery of being sick?" Good question. But imagine this scene: The worst criminal in history sits to eat at the king's table. The king serves him a meal, but the criminal can relax only if he knows he's pardoned. The only thing that can ease that kind of stress is simple trust that the king is good and that he'll always do what's best.

So I'm telling you that even if I'm enjoying life at the table of my King and God, I still know that my sins are huge and I deserve the worst. I think God appreciates it when we take sin seriously, when it turns our stomachs. To tell the truth, though, I don't mind that kind of suffering.

Wherever God takes you in life, be satisfied with His decision. You may think I'm happy, but in a way I envy you. I'd take pain and suffering any day if it was with the Lord. On the flip side, world-class pleasures would be no better than hell without Him—and only slightly better if I knew I was suffering for God.

Pretty soon I'll be going to God, standing before Him. I'd go through anything if I could just see Him for a moment. My comfort in this life is that I see Him by faith. Sometimes I can even say, "It's not just believing; it's seeing!" Faith has taught me to feel. With that kind of assurance, that kind of practice of faith, I live and die with Him.

So stay with God always. In the end, He's the only real support and comfort for you when you're sick. I'll pray for Him to stay by you.

Your servant,
Brother Lawrence

THE TWELFTH LETTER

ANYONE WANT TO KNOW GOD BETTER?
A THUMBNAIL SKETCH OF MY JOURNEY

My Dear Reverend Mother,

I know you're eager to hear how I've experienced the Lord's day-to-day closeness. So I'll explain to you this gift of God, but on one condition: that you show my letter to no one.* Otherwise I really couldn't write so freely to you, no matter how much I cared for your spiritual growth.

Actually, for me it started with confusion. I checked out all kinds of books, but each one gave a different approach to knowing God and living a spiritual life. The more opinions I found, the more I understood how they would just confuse me, rather than help me reach my goal. Because really, all I wanted was to live my life completely given to God. Period.

The good part was that all that bookish conflict drove me to a decision: I would give my all for *the* All. In other words, I decided to give everything I had for the One who *is* everything. Once that decision was behind me, the next step was to deal with all the junk, all the sin that cluttered my life. For the love of Jesus, I gave up everything but Him. I started fresh, living as if there were no one else in the world—no one but Jesus and me.

---

* This letter was not shared until after Brother Lawrence d⁻

Sometimes it seemed as though I was a criminal standing in front of God the Judge, waiting for my sentence. Other times, in my heart I saw Him as my Dad, my Father, my God. I praised Him as often as I could, and I kept my mind locked into the place where God was: His holy presence. If my mind wandered, I steered it back to that place. Staying with God became my primary goal, not just at scheduled prayer times, but in every hour and every minute. Even when I was busy working, I flushed out any thought that got between my Lord and me.

I've been doing this ever since I became a monk—maybe not 100 percent or perfectly, but I've gained so much. I owe everything I've gained to God's mercy and goodness because we (and especially I) can't do anything without Him.

Here's what happens: When we stay focused on God in His presence, it gets harder to disappoint Him or do things He doesn't want . . . at least on purpose. We discover a holy freedom to go to the Lord for everything we need—the breath to breathe for Him, the life to live for Him, the grace to keep going. After a while, with practice, being in God's presence this way becomes a totally natural habit.

Please thank God with me for His great goodness because I'll never be able to thank Him enough on my own. Me! A total loser. Never mind all the ways I've turned against Him. He's loved me anyway. So everyone, everywhere—praise Him! Amen!

Yours,
Brother Lawrence

ETERNAL SECURITY THROUGH LARGER-THAN-LIFE FAITH

November 28, 1690

Dear Reverend Mother,

We can expect to leave behind a lot of our physical problems the more we get used to practicing God's presence. Even so, God often lets us suffer a bit to help refine our souls and keep us close and dependent on Him. But my experience is that when we're close to God, we really don't suffer.

Don't give up; just give Him your pain and ask for strength to work through it. Above all, make thinking about God your number one habit. Don't forget Him. Tell Him how much you love Him even when you're sick or down. Volunteer your life to Him and then do it again. And when you're at your worst, humbly come to Him in love (just like a child to a parent) and tell Him this: "Your will be done in my life!" I'll try to help you with my humble prayers.

God can draw us to Himself in many ways. Though sometimes it seems as if He's hiding, we can be confident in Christ when we build on faith alone. With faith as our foundation, we invest everything in God. He never lets us down when we need Him.

So even though I have no idea where God is taking me or how much longer He'll let me live, I'm always happy. Though everyone suffers and I myself deserve heavy discipline, the joy just keeps coming. It's bubbling up so much I can hardly hold it back.

If God would let me share some of your pain, I'd be willing—except I'm so weak that if God left me even for a second, I'd instantly turn into the most pitiful person alive. I know He would never do that, of course—faith convinces me as much as reason or common sense. By faith I know He never abandons us, though we can turn from Him. We should fear even the thought of leaving Him. We should always stay with Him, living and dying in His presence.

Pray for me, as I pray for you.

Yours,
Brother Lawrence

THE FOURTEENTH LETTER

SUFFERING HURTS BUT
BRINGS US CLOSER TO GOD

December 21, 1690

My Good Reverend Mother,

I'm sorry to see you suffering this long, but it does make me feel better to know that through your trouble we see proof of God's love for you. If you look at your pains that way, they'll be easier to bear.

I think in your case, you should forget the useless human remedies and submit totally to God's care.* Perhaps God is just waiting for that kind of surrender and faith to cure you. Considering that you've done all you humanly can and are still growing sicker, don't wait any longer. You wouldn't be tempting God by putting yourself completely in His hands and expecting everything from Him.

Remember in my last letter how I told you that God sometimes allows physical sickness, working through it to cure a sick soul. So hang in there and don't ask God to take away the pain. Instead, remember how much you love Him

---

* Editor's note: Readers should keep in mind how little the primitive state of the medical arts offered in the seventeenth century, though the principle of relying ultimately on God for healing remains the same today.

and then ask for strength to bear all that He wants for as long as He decides. At first that's a very tough prayer, but eventually it turns sweet when our hearts are right with God. He appreciates it too.

Love sweetens pain. When we love God and are fixed on Him no matter what, we discover deep joy and courage as we suffer for Him. That's the pattern to follow. Please do! Make God your Comforter, your Healer. After all, He's the only Doctor for all that ails us. He's the Father of the afflicted, the sick, and the disabled—and He's always ready to help us. He loves us so, so much more than we could ever think or imagine. So love Him only; don't look for His comfort anywhere else. I hope He reassures you soon. Adieu.

I'll help with my poor, simple prayers.

Yours always in the Lord,
Brother Lawrence

THE FIFTEENTH LETTER

STILL WAITING ON GOD?
KEEP KNOCKING ON THE DOOR

January 22, 1691

My Very Dear Reverend Mother,

Praise God that He relieved you from your pain a bit, just the way you asked. I've almost died a few times myself and felt during those times that I'd never been happier. Those were the times I didn't pray for relief, but rather for strength to suffer with courage, a humble spirit, and love.

No matter how much you have to struggle, accept everything God gives you with love. It's so sweet to suffer with God! Paradise, really. If we want to enjoy paradise-peace in this life, we have to get used to walking and talking with God. It's a familiar walk, as with a friend. A humble walk because He's God and we're not. A loving conversation with God because He wants to talk with us on the way.

But we need to check our spirits—always hold them back from wandering away from Him. We need to build our hearts into spiritual temples so we always have a place to adore Him, to tell Him how much we love Him. We need to keep a close eye on our lives so we don't do, say, or think things He won't be happy with. Then, when God fills our hearts and minds to overflowing, suffering fills with comfort.

I know the first part of this road is rough because we don't see where we're going as we step out purely by faith. But even though it's hard, we also know we can do all things through God's grace. He never says no to those who ask with their whole hearts. So knock on God's door and keep knocking. Believe me, in His time He will open the door and pour out His grace on you. He'll grant you all at once what you've been waiting on for many years.

Adieu. Pray for me, as I pray for you. I hope to see God soon.

Yours in the Lord,
Brother Lawrence

THE SIXTEENTH LETTER

THE WAY HOME:
BROTHER LAWRENCE'S LAST THOUGHTS

February 6, 1691

My Good Reverend Mother,

No one knows what we need better than God does, and He always has our best in mind. If we only understood just how much He loves us, we'd always be ready to accept both the bitter and the sweet from His hand. In the end, there really would be no difference between the two because we'd be satisfied with anything that came from the Lord.

We think we can't handle the worst troubles only because we see them in the wrong light. It's totally different, though, when we recognize that they come from God's hand. When we understand how our loving Father keeps us humble or in a place where we'll look to Him, then our sufferings turn from bitter to sweet. A bad experience might even bring comfort.

So we should channel all our time and effort into knowing God. The more we know Him, the more we want to know Him better. After a time, we can basically measure how much we love Him by how much we've come to know Him. Our love grows greater as we go deeper in our relationship with Him. It follows, then, that if we love God deeply, we'll love Him just as much when we're in pain as we do when we're having a party.

It's not good enough to follow God (or even say we love Him) just because of the favors He can do for us. No matter how good those favors are, they can never take us as close to God as one simple act of faith can. So let's look to Him all the time—but in faith. Because we're believers, He lives in us, so we don't need to look outside ourselves or anywhere else to find Him.

Shame on us for being rude by ignoring God because we're busy with so many little things that don't please Him and may even offend Him. He may put up with it for now, but one day it will cost us.

Let's get serious about dedicating ourselves to God, first by clearing out our hearts and minds for Him. He wants our whole hearts. If we ask Him and do our part, pretty soon we'll see the changes in our lives that we hope for.

I'm still so thankful for the way He's helped you feel better. For me, I'm hoping God in His mercy will bring me to see Him in a few days.* Let's pray for each other.

> *In Christ,*
> *Brother Lawrence*

---

* God granted Brother Lawrence's final wishes. Six days after this letter was written, he died and went to be with the Lord.

Part 3:

SPIRITUAL SAYINGS OF

Brother Lawrence

THESE SAYINGS, or maxims, were originally written by Brother Lawrence probably after he wrote some of his famous letters. Why do we think so? Though many of the concepts are similar to those presented in his letters, they're distilled and refined and carefully arranged by topic. They reflect someone who's had a chance to think about his faith and his all-consuming desire to practice God's presence, as well as to encourage others to do the same. Here are his thoughts.

FAITH, HOPE, AND LOVE

Everything is possible for those who believe, more for those who hope, still more for those who love, and most of all for those who faithfully combine all three: faith, hope, and love. Being baptized and believing in Christ are the first steps to spiritual maturity. But to reach the goal, follow these principles faithfully:

1. **Look for God's hand in everything** and give Him the credit in all that you say and do. Our goal should be to serve as His number one cheerleaders in this life because that's what we hope to be in heaven. In the process, look to Him for help in getting past the rough spots in the Christian walk.

2. **Don't expect the road to be easy.** If we take a good look at ourselves, we find we don't look too good. We're sinners who deserve the worst; we're not worthy of Christ's name. On top of that, life drags us down, and our health sometimes suffers. The bottom line is that God sometimes needs to humble us, to remind us of who we really are.

3. **Remember that bad days are for our good.** God is looking for living sacrifices. He's still in charge when we find ourselves in miserable situations—suffering, tempted, or worse. He will keep us there as long as He sees fit because unless we truly learn to submit our hearts and minds to God's will, we'll never grow up to become fully devoted believers.

4. **The more we want to grow, the more we depend on God's grace.** Our souls would be totally shipwrecked without Him. In fact, the outside world, human nature, and Satan combine to assault us. It's a fierce triple threat that never lets up. It would sweep away our souls if we weren't anchored in Christ, dependent on Him.

Living a Spiritual Life

1. **Get used to it.** Above all else, the main ingredient of a genuine spiritual life is practicing God's presence — living for God's closeness, day by day; getting used to spending time with Him; and praying to Him humbly (remember who you are!) and with love (remember who He is!). Keep praying always, every moment — no rules, no systems. Just keep praying, especially when you're tempted or down, when you're feeling spiritually dry, or when you don't know what to say. Even if you're disgusted with something, if you're unfaithful to Him, or if you've sinned, pray!

2. **Turn doing into praying.** We need to keep practicing so that every little thing we do is turned into a prayer, a little conversation with God. That doesn't mean following some kind of blueprint. It does mean doing and praying from a pure and simple heart, without a lot of clutter.

3. **Keep your eyes open.** We need to keep a close watch on how we act, making sure we don't do something rash or stupid during the times when we're stressed

out. Instead, we should relax and work with God in a peaceful and loving way and then beg Him to accept our work. By staying tight with God this way, we crush the head of the devil and make his weapons fall from his hands.

4. **Take a break.** When we're busy with work or daily life, during our devotional reading time, or even during church services, we should pause for a moment, as often as we can, just to tell God we love Him with our whole hearts. It's sort of like we're secretly enjoying the fragrance of His goodness as He passes by. Because you know God lives in your deepest heart and soul, why not clear your calendar for Him once in a while—even put aside your spoken prayers—just to adore Him quietly, praise Him, ask Him for what you need, offer Him your devotion, or tell Him thank you? God loves it when we take this kind of mini-retreat during the day, when we leave behind our agendas to adore Him in our hearts. What's more, these retreats free us step-by-step as they destroy the kind of self-love that flourishes when we're out in the world. In the end, the best way we can tell God we're faithful is to turn away (and keep turning away) from material things—just so we can be with our Creator for one moment.

I'm not saying you should turn away from everything you're doing. That's impossible. Let wisdom and good common sense guide you because they're the mother of virtues. That said, know that even people who are seeking God make a common mistake: They don't leave the world's things far enough behind so they can just adore God from the inside out and soak in the warm peace of His presence.

I did get off the track here for a little while, but I thought it was worth mentioning. Let's get back to our principles.

5. **Love by faith.** Faith powers our worship. When we love and adore God, everything begins and ends with faith, even as we remember that:

- God really lives in our hearts and lives.
- We need to worship and serve Him "in spirit and truth" (John 4:23, NIV).
- He sees everything that happens or will ever happen.
- He is above all, and everything that lives depends on Him.
- He is infinitely perfect, infinitely excellent, and totally in charge.

That means God deserves our all, our total surrender. For that matter, He deserves everything we can imagine in heaven or earth. He can do whatever He likes with it anytime He wants to. So really it's only fair that we owe Him everything we think, say, or do. Let's be sure we pay up.

6. **Take a closer look.** It's important to look at ourselves to learn our weaknesses, where we need to grow, and which qualities will be the hardest to develop. We also need to be aware of the sin traps we might tend to fall into, where they are, and why they tempt us. When we're tempted, we need God's direct number so we can flee to Him without hesitating. We need to stand firm on God's majesty, humbly give Him our love, tell Him what's wrong, and then ask Him for His gracious support. When we do, we'll discover in God every virtue or quality we need.

Love God in Spirit and Truth

There are three points to consider here:

1. To really love God in spirit and truth means to adore God the way we're made to. Because God is a spirit, it follows that we have to worship Him in spirit and truth. In other words, we love Him from the core of our souls. We bow before Him willingly (no one is making us) and humbly (we know our place as sinners). Only God can recognize what's really behind this kind of worship, what's in our hearts. If we worship Him this way often enough, it will become so natural we'll feel as if God is one with our souls and our souls are one with God. The more we practice, the more we'll understand.

2. Worshiping God in truth means knowing Him for who He is, especially compared to who we are. It means knowing Him truly and certainly with all our hearts and knowing that He is who He says He is: perfect beyond perfect, worthy of our love, and infinitely removed from sin and evil . . . and the list goes on. It's

hard to see how anyone with half a brain wouldn't fall down and worship this awesome God.

3. Worshiping God in truth is confessing that there's a grand canyon between Him and us, but that if we say yes to Him, He'll make us more like Him. Who would make the huge mistake of holding back—even for a second—the respect, love, service, and nonstop worship we owe Him?

Getting Closer to God

The soul can be linked with God in three ways: general, virtual, and actual.

1. General union is when grace alone draws us to God. Grace is unexpected; we don't deserve it.
2. Virtual union with God lasts only as long as a special effort or event. It's a one-time happening.
3. Actual union is by far the best—the real thing. The soul doesn't just sit back and soak it all in like a sponge or a spectator, as in the other two ways. Believe me, it moves! It's more fiery than an open flame, brighter than the midday sun on a cloudless day.

    Even so, the feelings that come with actual union can be tricky. We're not talking about basic heart emotions, the kind we display when we blurt out something such as, "I love You, Lord, with all my heart!" Not quite. It's hard to explain, but this is a deep soul experience. It's sweet and peaceful, from the spirit. It bows before God and falls on its face with a humble heart. It's full of love but at the same time completely uncluttered. Actual union lifts the soul up to a place where we have no choice but to love God, worship Him, and hold on to Him with tender hugs I can't even describe. You have to actually feel it to understand what I'm talking about.

Watch out, though! Everyone who wants to know God deeply should be aware of attractive distractions that can sidetrack the will and hijack our good intentions. Admit it: No one can fully understand God. But if we ever really want to be united with Him, we need to pull back from all kinds of other pleasures—spiritual as well as worldly. We need to strip our wills down to the basics so they can steer us straight toward loving God above everything else. If we're ever going to succeed, it will only be because we're motivated by love alone.

It comes down to a question of will. Keep in mind there can be a huge difference between what we'd like to do and what we end up doing. But the will—our decision-making tool—is defined and limited by the soul. The soul operating on love finds its only true destination—in God.

THE PRESENCE OF GOD

What is the presence of God? It's when we focus our spirits on the Lord or when we realize He's right here with us. It can happen through our imaginations or understandings.

I know a man who has practiced the presence of God for the past forty years.* He understands what it means to be in the presence of God, though he has several names for it:

- A simple act
- A clear, distinct way to know God
- A fuzzy vision
- A loving gaze
- Waiting on God
- Silent chats with God
- Soul peace

They're all just different names for the same thing, he told me—synonyms for practicing God's presence. Then he described for me how this state of being has become natural for him.

---

* Once again, Brother Lawrence is being modest and is talking about himself in the third person—just like in the first letter.

He often calls his mind into God's presence as soon as he's done with his workday—and often while he's still in the middle of things. He just lifts his heart of hearts to the Lord. It's no work at all to do this, no effort; it just happens out of habit. But his very heart and soul are held up to the heights of God, who is his rest and the bull's-eye of his soul.

My friend calls this the actual presence of God, though it includes all the other flavors of God's presence as well. Backed up by faith, his soul is nearly always satisfied in Christ. He now lives as if he and God were the only ones alive on the whole planet. He's constantly talking with the Lord, asking for what he needs, celebrating with God in too many ways to count.

I should point out that this conversation with God is going on in the deepest reaches of my friend's heart—the center of his soul. That's where our souls talk to God, heart to heart, bringing the deepest peace we can imagine. When that happens, everything outside seems no more important than a brief flash of cheap fireworks. These things of the world hardly ever cause a ripple or disturb our inner peace.

But back to what I was saying about the presence of God: Let me tell you that God's sweet, loving attention quietly sparks a little divine fire in the soul. Get closer to embrace the Lord and that spark will explode into such a holy bonfire that you'll have to put a lid on it to keep the feelings under control!

We'd be surprised to know what really goes on between the soul and God. He seems so pleased with the back-and-forth communion that He showers blessings on those who commit themselves to Him. As if God were concerned we'd return to the world, He sets a banquet table overflowing with spiritual food—far beyond what we could ever ask for. And we do nothing to bring it on or make it happen. All we really do is say yes to God.

So God's presence is health food for the soul. God's presence is life itself. It's showered on us even though we don't deserve it.

FINDING GOD'S PRESENCE

1. First, you need to guard yourselves from doing, saying, or thinking anything that would offend God, and you need to keep a short account with Him. If you slip, go straight to Him and ask for His forgiveness. We're talking about purity of life.
2. Next, you need to keep your heart's eye focused on God always, remembering in love to stay quiet and humble before Him and not let your worries or day-to-day problems get in the way or drag you off the path.
3. In addition, you need to warm up your spiritual muscles and focus on the Lord before you begin any daily chores or regular work. That way you'll stay fixed on Him all the way through it and afterward. But don't get discouraged; it takes a long while and a lot of hard work to develop this kind of habit. Once you've got it, though, a great abundance of joy comes to live in your life.

Doesn't it make sense that our hearts would be the first and the last to love and worship God, because the heart begins and ends all that we do? After all, the heart—the center of life—powers the rest of our bodies. The heart sets the pace, spiritual and otherwise. So it's the heart that lets us focus on God from within in a way that's natural and simple, without a fancy plan or a complicated agenda.

4. When you're coming into God's presence, I'd suggest you describe your feelings in a few words such as "I'm all Yours, Lord," "God of love, I love You with all my heart," or "Mold my heart to match Yours, God." Or tell God in your own way on the spur of the moment how you love Him—whatever works for you.

   In the process, though, be careful not to let your mind wander back to thinking about everyday things. Stay close to God so your will can keep your mind in line, focused on the Lord.

5. Working into this kind of presence of God is tough at first—painful, even. But with a little practice, this habit will secretly start doing its thing in your soul with incredible results. It'll draw down showers of God's grace and oh-so-quietly lead you right back to that simple, 360-degree view of God. That kind of holy contact with the Lord is the most real, yet the easiest kind of prayer anyone can pray. It's a prayer bursting with life.

6. Remember that drawing this close to God takes denial—saying no to stuffing our lives full of everything the world has to offer. Cut the umbilical cord! No one who is still attached to worldly pleasures can find full joy with God.

BENEFITS OF GOD'S PRESENCE

What is the first benefit of God's presence in our souls? Faith comes alive and steers everything we do in life. We'll notice the difference especially during the hard times, because the presence of God makes a way for His grace to start working in us when we're tempted or when we run into those unavoidable people problems.

Through this practice, the soul gets used to operating on faith, and then all it takes is a simple act of remembering to see and feel God's presence. We then can also freely and effectively call on God—and naturally He supplies our needs. So you could say that faith opens the door to a place of blessing, and the more the soul moves ahead, the more faith comes alive. Eventually this faith soaks through the soul to the point where we can almost say, "This isn't just a belief anymore. Now I actually see and experience God!"

Practicing God's presence puts meat on the bones of our hope as our hope grows to match what we learn about the Lord. In the process of helping us understand the mysteries of God, hope also turns a spotlight on the absolute beauty of God—far and away more captivating than any other beauty here on earth or in heaven. So our hope grows stronger, built up and encouraged by the majesty we seek and even now enjoy just a little.

Practicing God's presence sets up our wills to reject what the world has to offer, so we can say, "No thanks!" It also lights up our wills with God's loving, holy fire—a flame that reduces our opposition to toast. But a soul that does catch on fire can live only in God's presence from then on. That kind of presence also plants a holy missionary intensity in the heart—a sacred, passionate hope that everyone on the planet will come to know, love, serve, and worship the Lord.

By practicing God's presence and focusing on the Lord, our souls get to know Him so well that our days are spent serving Him in love, prayer, worship, and confession. Sometimes it all blends into one act of ongoing worship because our souls are locked into spending time with God.

You won't find many people who have reached this place, though, because God grants His special grace only to a few chosen souls. Being able to simply focus on God is actually a free gift from Him. If that sounds good to you but you're not sure if God has given you the ultimate gift, don't feel bad. He usually grants this special closeness to those who really want it. And if He doesn't grant it to you, just practice God's presence and be happy with the grace He gives all Christians. That will help you take your relationship with the Lord and your prayer life to a place that's nearly the same as what I've described.

Part 4:

IDEAS FOR PRACTICING THE PRESENCE

THIS SECTION provides real-life, practical ideas on how we can begin to practice God's presence in our lives today.

PRACTICING THE PRESENCE

Not many of us are monks, and none of us live in the seventeenth century. So at the end of this inspiring read, the question remains: How can we put modern wheels to the advice of Brother Lawrence? Given the breakneck pace of our lives today, can we *really* make it work?

Brother Lawrence would not have wanted a complicated answer to such a basic question. "What we need," wrote Multnomah Bible College professor Pamela Reeve, "are simple, practical, clear suggestions on how to practice God's presence."[7]

Amen. So let's begin at the workplace. In her book *Enjoying the Presence of God*, Jan Johnson tells a story of a woman working at a repetitive electronics assembly job. In between tasks, she takes a moment to pray for the worker next to her, a quick word to God asking how she can help in her coworker's life. She ponders that prayer the rest of the afternoon, wondering why she's praying but keeping an ongoing conversation with the Lord.

Soon she sees her answer as that coworker shares her own faith with several other workers during a break the following day. She'd been praying for a missionary![8]

And so it goes. We wonder if it's possible to really practice God's presence 24/7, the way the apostle Paul said we should. How do we "pray hard and long" (Ephesians 6:18) or "pray all the time" (1 Thessalonians 5:17)?

All the time? Don't worry if that sounds intimidating. Let's look first at what that kind of prayer is not. It's not unnatural. It's not a secret formula. And it's not an introspective, contemplative dead end.

On the other hand, practicing God's presence in our work and lives has to be no less natural than it was for Brother Lawrence in his busy monastery kitchen. Out loud or silent, long or short.

Part of the answer lies in looking to God the way the electronics worker did—looking outward, searching for needs the way our Father does. That helps us line up our wills with His and keep the focus off ourselves. So try this: The next time you're faced with a few minutes of downtime, start praying for the people around you. Waiting for an oil change? Pray for the mechanic or the receptionist. Stuck in traffic? Pray for the sleepy-looking truck driver coming up behind you. In the supermarket checkout line? Pray for the harried checker who needs encouragement. Before long, you'll find opportunities all around you.

Such prayers don't always have to be eloquent, wordy, or even end with "in Jesus' name, amen." Jesus knows your heart. For example, "I'm all Yours, Lord" is just four words, but we can use that simple prayer to tell God we're trusting Him as we go into surgery. In the same way, quick prayers such as "Please fix his heart" can touch real needs. So can "Show me how to change" or even just "Thank You, Lord."

Sound too simple? It might, but it's not. These are "bullet" prayers, "breath" prayers, "arrow" prayers—call them whatever you like. They won't necessarily replace your other prayer times, but we're talking about how to stay close to God the *rest* of your day, not just during formal or scripted prayer times.

Don't know how to pray for someone? Join the club. Then take another look at God's Word because He's already loaded it up with great examples. You can pray that a person would come to "live creatively," as it says in Galatians 6:1, or that God would help you step into a "generous common life with those who have trained you" (Galatians 6:6). The Scriptures are chock-full of these kinds of prayer helps. Pick out a couple of verses and try them for yourself and others throughout the day.

That's the beauty of it. God's presence is only a thought or prayer away. It never has to stop. We hang up the phone after politely turning down a solicitor for a local charity. How can we pray for that person? We talk to our child's teacher who's struggling with a lively class, a boss who's just lost a spouse, the bus driver who's sick. God has a plan for all of them. Use everyday life as a call to on-the-spot, immediate prayer.

Sure, we could write down their names on our list and pray for them the next morning. That's certainly not a bad idea. But why wait? And why wait to thank the Lord for the rain, for the car that started, or for the baby that smiled? Why wait to tell our heavenly Father "I love You" or "Here's my tax report, Lord. I want every number to honor You"?

When we offer this kind of spontaneous prayer, God says that the things we do—offered in a spirit of devotion—become part of the prayer itself.[9] Brother Lawrence wrote about this kind of prayer. Though that may sound mystical, it's really not. When we pray like this, we find that we're on the way to praying "all the time," as Paul taught.

Of course we forget to pray, and that's a good reason for setting up little reminders to ourselves. I try to pray for the U.S. president and his family ("for kings and all those in authority" [1 Timothy 2:2, NIV]) every time he appears on the television news. You can set up your own reminders for your own arrow prayers.

These are the kinds of prayers that will eventually come naturally, almost without thinking. They are the kinds of prayers we need to cultivate. Even so, as we direct our prayers to God throughout the day, we needn't take the easy way, the most comfortable way. Some of these prayers may actually be downright uncomfortable—prayers for people who annoy us, for children who break our best china, or for leaders of groups we disagree with (and *not*, "God, strike 'em down!").

Just as we pray for people who challenge us, we can pray for ourselves in difficult times. God is certainly big enough to hear us in our times of grief and pain, anguish and worry. He is big enough to handle our questions, so ask away. That's part of the daily give-and-take of a more intimate prayer life with the Savior.

While you're at it, try asking to see things from God's perspective, whether you're reading the paper or watching the news, bowling with friends or trying to survive another day at the office. Try this prayer, originally penned by missionary Amy Carmichael:

> "Holy Spirit
> think through me
> till your ideas
> are my ideas."[10]

Often God's ideas are going to be centered around Jesus and others—not around the person praying. After all, God is in the business of redeeming the world, not just our little corner of it. So if you start praying that prayer, watch out. He may gently point out areas of your life that need changing. That's a good start. Or He may answer your requests with, "Go ahead. Let's go try something new. Let's step out."

Practicing God's presence like this isn't meant to replace our times of worship, our Bible study, or our devotions. But it can breathe new life into our entire approach to the living God. He wants to share our every thought, our every moment. The more we learn this discipline of everyday communion with God, the closer we'll get to His heart and His desire for our lives.

And isn't that what we all want?

These additional resources can help you practice God's presence in your everyday life:

Baker, Howard. *Soul Keeping.* Colorado Springs, Colo.: NavPress, 1998.

Brown, M. Wayne. *Water from Stone.* Colorado Springs, Colo.: NavPress, 2004.

Imbach, Jeff. *The River Within.* Colorado Springs, Colo.: NavPress, 1998.

Johnson, Jan. *Enjoying the Presence of God.* Colorado Springs, Colo.: NavPress, 1996.

———. *Savoring God's Word.* Colorado Springs, Colo.: NavPress, 2004.

Notes

1. Hannah Whitall Smith, introduction to Brother Lawrence, *The Practice of the Presence of God the Best Rule of a Holy Life: Being Conversations and Letters of Nicholas Herman of Lorraine (Brother Lawrence)*, trans. (New York: Revell, 1895), p. iii.

2. Brother Lawrence of the Resurrection, *The Practice of the Presence of God*, trans. (New York: Image-Doubleday, 1977), p. xxi.

3. Tozer, A. W., *The Price of Neglect*, comp. Harry Verploegh (Camp Hill, Pa.: Christian Publications, 1991), p. 22.

4. Scott Larsen, ed., *Indelible Ink* (Colorado Springs, Colo.: WaterBrook, 2003), pp. 243, 253, 270.

5. Tozer, p. 22.

6. Discalced Carmelites, "Br. Lawrence of the Resurrection," *Our Carmelite Saints*, http://www.carmelite.com/saints/lawrence.html (accessed August 10, 2004).

7. Pamela Reeve, endorsement for *Enjoying the Presence of God*, by Jan Johnson (Colorado Springs, Colo.: NavPress, 1996), p. 4.

8. Johnson, p. 14.

9. Johnson, p. 43.

10. Amy Carmichael, "Think Through Me," *Eerdman's Book of Famous Prayers*, ed. Veronica Zundel (Grand Rapids, Mich.: Eerdmans, 1983), p. 69.

ABOUT ROBERT ELMER

ROBERT ELMER (www.RobertElmerBooks.com) has over twenty-five years of experience as a news editor and reporter, freelance writer and advertising copywriter, assistant pastor, workshop leader, and novelist. He is a graduate of Simpson College and St. Mary's College in California. Most recently, he is the author of *The Duet* and *The Celebrity*, as well as over thirty-five popular novels for younger readers. He and his wife, Ronda, are the parents of three young adults and live in the Pacific Northwest.

MORE RESOURCES TO DRAW YOU CLOSER TO THE HEART OF GOD.

The Rabbi's Heartbeat
Brennan Manning
1-57683-469-7

Best-selling author Brennan Manning challenges readers of all ages to become real with Christ and live their lives without hiding or posing as perfect. This book is a daily reminder to live as we really are—God's beloved children.

The Pursuit of Holiness
25th Anniversary Edition
Jerry Bridges
1-57683-463-8

Twenty-five years ago, *The Pursuit of Holiness* opened Christians' eyes to a new perspective on holiness— finally it became tangible and not some utopian dream. Today, this book is as relevant as ever because the pursuit of holiness never ends. It is a marathon race to the finish, from our first days as Christians to our last. So, read it again. Get inspired again.

To order copies, visit your local Christian bookstore,
call NavPress at 1-800-366-7788,
or log on to www.navpress.com.

To locate a Christian bookstore near you,
call 1-800-991-7747.

BRINGING TRUTH TO LIFE
www.navpress.com